Rescue
at Blue Canyon

Written by Mary-Anne Creasy

Illustrated by Omar Aranda

Flying Start
to Literacy®

Contents

Chapter 1

Traffic jam

Victor knocked on Tammy's door.

"Come on, Tammy, are you ready?"

Victor looked at his reflection in the window, then brushed the invisible crumbs off his jacket and adjusted his tie. Tammy burst through the door, laughing.

"I can see you through the window, Victor. You're so in love with that uniform!"

Victor looked embarrassed. "Yeah, I know – I'll get used to it."

Tammy smiled. "I think it's great you're so excited. I remember my first day as a park ranger. It was the best day."

Tammy found the car keys and bounded down the stairs. The gravel crunched under her boots as she walked to the car. She breathed deeply, looking up at the blue sky between the new green leaves.

"Yep, I think spring is here," she said as she kicked a pile of crusty snow. "Finally, a warm, sunny day!"

"I wonder if there will be a lot of visitors in the park today," said Victor as they started down the road. Victor had spent the past two weeks learning all about Blue Canyon National Park, its animals and geological features, and how to do rock-face rescues on its dangerous cliffs. He was excited to meet his first visitors and guide them around the park.

"I doubt there will be many visitors. The park opened just last week and hardly anyone came," said Tammy. "But we have work to do. Remember the earth tremour last week? We have to make sure that some of the remote areas of the park are still safe before the summer season. It's our job to keep people safe and make sure they know the rules."

They drove towards the mountains where the road rose up to the towering, rocky cliffs.

Suddenly, Tammy braked. A long line of cars had pulled over on the side of the road.

"What's going on?" said Tammy.

They drove past the cars, but as they rounded a bend, they could see even more cars pulling over and stopping. People were getting out and walking towards the forest.

"This is weird!" said Tammy, puzzled. "We shouldn't see so many cars this time of year."

"Maybe some of the park's wildlife have wandered onto the road!" said Victor, excited.

In the park ranger training course, he had learnt what to do if animals wandered onto the road or if people suddenly stopped to look at the wildlife nearby. Cars would stop, causing a traffic jam. In summer, one of these jams could block the traffic for hours.

But Tammy and Victor couldn't see any animals.

"That's odd," said Victor. "All these people are looking at their phones as they're walking towards that track."

"That's the way up to Canyon View," said Tammy curiously, as she pulled the car over.

Victor's phone pinged. "Oh wow, Tammy, take a look at this."

A young man was doing a jumping jack on a rocky ledge that jutted out over the steep canyon.

"We have a problem," said Tammy. "It's not safe up there."

"How come?" asked Victor.

"When the earth tremour happened last week, some of the cliff under the ledge must have fallen away," said Tammy. "That's why it's jutting out like that. More of the cliff face could fall away at any moment. That hiker obviously came in a couple of days ago and posted this photo."

"What do we do?"

"Come on, Victor, it's time for your first effort at crowd control."

They quickly got out of the car and followed the crowd striding up the hillside.

Chapter 2

A bad fall

"Help, help!" a woman called as she came running down the track towards Tammy and Victor. "A boy has slipped off the cliff! He's stuck on a ledge. He can't move and he can't climb back up."

"We'll need a rescue team," said Tammy. "Victor, go on ahead and see what's happened. I'll contact the ranger station."

Victor struggled to pass the crowd along the steep track, but after about ten minutes, he was close to the top of the ridge. As he emerged from the forest, the bright sun almost blinded him.

A bunch of people was taking photos of the rocky ledge that jutted out over the canyon. It was what remained of the cliff that had fallen away and it stretched out like a jagged hand over the canyon far below.

Victor gazed in wonder at it. It was the photo that had been posted online and the thing all these people had come to see. People were also crowded along the edge of the canyon, talking and filming on their phones. A man was lying on his stomach, reaching down, over the edge.

"It's okay, Jacob. Just stay still. The park ranger is coming," the man said.

As Victor moved closer to the edge of the canyon, his legs began to shake. A memory from his childhood flashed in his mind.

Victor was back in the tree at his grandma's farm. He was nine years old and his pet iguana, Iggy, had escaped and climbed to the top of the tree. Victor's big brother, Jim, said not to worry, that he would climb up and rescue Iggy.

Victor watched Jim climb higher and higher. It looked so easy, so he climbed up after him. When he could go no further, he stopped and looked down. The ground was spinning and zoomed up towards him.

Jim had the iguana in one hand and he called down to Victor. "What are you doing up here? I can't climb down with you in the way. Climb down!"

But Victor was frozen. He squeezed his eyes shut. He could not move.

"Officer, please help! My son has fallen!" the man said.

Victor took a deep breath and opened his eyes. He got down on his hands knees and peered over the edge of the canyon. The boy, Jacob, was lying on a rocky ledge, several metres below the edge of the cliff. The ledge had saved his fall. He was clinging to a rock and crying.

The man was reaching down to be closer to his son.

"Dad, I'm scared!"

"It's okay, Jacob. I'm here," said the father, trying to sound calm.

Another wave of dizziness washed over Victor. As the ground below zoomed in and out, he squeezed his eyes shut.

The father turned to Victor. "Can't you go down and get him?"

"We have to wait for the rescue team, sir. My partner has called in to the ranger station. I can't rescue Jacob by myself and not without equipment."

Where is Tammy? Victor wished that he had gone back to the car to call in the rescue team and that Tammy was there instead of him – she would know what to do.

Chapter 3
Emergency

Suddenly, there was a loud whistle. *Peewwwwt!*

"Okay, everyone, we have an emergency situation here.
I need everyone to please move away from the edge of the
canyon. It's not safe," Tammy said in a loud voice.

Victor took the rescue kit from Tammy and quickly unpacked
it. *Stay busy*, he told himself. In the park ranger training
course, he had learnt how to do a rock-face rescue. He just
had to remember.

He focused his mind on the small, specific tasks of laying out the harness, rope, first-aid kit and heat blanket, ready for the rescue team.

"It's okay, Jacob, we'll have you out soon. You just have to stay still," said Tammy. She noticed Victor's pale face. "Are you all right?"

Victor nodded. Was it that obvious that he was nervous? He couldn't let Tammy know. "I'm just worried about Jacob."

Tammy lowered her voice and said, "It's too dangerous for us to rescue Jacob by ourselves. We have to wait for the rescue team. Keep Jacob calm and relaxed. I'm going back down the road to meet the rescue team and guide them here. I hope it doesn't take long. I don't like the look of the sky."

As Victor glanced at the horizon, a blanket of dark clouds moved up the canyon. He crawled back to the edge of the cliff and called down to Jacob.

Just don't look down, he told himself.

Jacob's frightened face looked up at Victor, who knew exactly how Jacob was feeling.

Victor remembered when he was high up in the tree, with his arms wrapped tightly around a branch. The branch was slippery and he felt himself sliding.

"Victor, look up at me!" shouted his brother. "I'll help you!"

Victor gasped. "I can't. I can't move. I'm going to fall."

"It's okay, I'm coming down to help you," said Jim, and he climbed down till he reached Victor.

Jim was still holding the iguana, which was gripping his hand.

"I'm going to have to let go of Iggy to help you. He might escape again, but don't worry. We'll find him. We just have to get you down."

Victor opened eyes. His brother placed Iggy on a branch.

"Now, grab my hand," said Jim.

Victor took a deep breath and the dizziness passed. He put on a cheerful voice.

"Hey, Jacob, how did you get down there? That looks a bit tricky."

Jacob stopped crying and looked up. "We were jumping for a photo, and I landed funny and fell backwards. I lost my balance and started to slip. I caught hold of this rock and that's when I stopped slipping."

"Sorry, Jake, my fault," said the dad, looking guilty.

Victor told Jacob about the many things in the park that he should check out during his next visit. He tried to keep his eyes on Jacob and not on the ground far below them.

Victor's walkie-talkie crackled with the sound of Tammy's voice.

"Go ahead, Tammy," said Victor.

"The rescue team can't get through. More cars have arrived and the road is blocked at least one kilometre back. A rescue team is coming in the helicopter, but it won't be there for twenty minutes."

A sudden gust of wind made everyone look up. Victor saw dark clouds gathering.

"It looks like a storm is coming!" said Victor into the walkie-talkie. "I need you back up here. The clouds are drifting up the canyon and we could lose visibility."

"I'm on my way back up to you. Over!" said Tammy.

Victor looked down at Jacob. He was shivering with fear as the clouds swirled around him.

Suddenly, to Victor's relief, Tammy was by his side.

"How's it going?" She looked down and saw Jacob was still clinging to the rock in terror. Then she looked up at the darkening sky. They were running out of time.

Tammy's walkie-talkie crackled.

"Base to Ranger Tammy! Looks like the weather's going to stop us from getting up there to rescue Jacob in the helicopter. The wind is too strong. It's just too dangerous."

Jacob's father saw Tammy and Victor exchange a worried look, and the colour drained from the man's face.

"What's happening?" he asked, sounding desperate. "How are we going to rescue my son?!"

"Dad, Dad, is anybody coming?" called Jacob, shaking with fear.

Victor knew he didn't have a choice – a plan took shape in his mind. *I have to get Jacob off that rock and I need to do it now,* he told himself.

Chapter 4

Rescue

"Jacob, hold tight! We're coming down and we will bring you back up here," called Tammy.

Tammy grabbed Victor's arm. "I know this is your first day, but you've done the training. If you want to be a ranger this is something you're going to have to do."

Victor was scared, but he didn't want Tammy to see. He took a deep breath. If he was going to be a park ranger, he would have to face his fear.

"I can do this," he said. He pulled on the harness and then shackled it to the rope. Tammy took one end and tied it expertly to a tree.

"I need some strong people to help lower Victor down to the ledge," she said. "There's a storm coming, so we need to rescue the boy now!"

Victor was at the edge of the cliff. The canyon was
filled with a swirling cloud and he could no longer see the
canyon floor.

Suddenly, a gust of wind parted the cloud and he could see
the canyon floor far below. Victor felt himself swaying as
he stood. Everyone was busy lining up to grab the rope,
so no one noticed.

"Grab my hand," said Jim.

"I can't – I'll fall!"

"I'll hold your arm so you won't fall. It's okay – I'm strong."

Victor was terrified. He squeezed the branch tightly, but he could feel his arms getting weak. Jim gripped his arm.

"Let go. I've got you!"

Victor's arms suddenly gave way. He was dangling in the air, his brother gripping his arm tightly. But Jim's hand was slick with sweat.

"I'm slipping!" screamed Victor.

It was then that Jim lost his grip. Victor fell through the air and landed with a thud. He felt an intense pain in his arm. It was broken. Jim quickly scampered down the tree and helped him. Victor was rushed to the hospital and his arm was put in a plaster cast.

Although Victor's arm eventually healed, he never forgot how terrified he felt as he fell through the air.

This is different, Victor told himself. *It wasn't Jim's fault. I'll be okay.* He looked at the determined faces of the people holding the rope. They wouldn't let him down. They wouldn't drop him.

He crouched at the edge of the canyon and shouted down to Jacob.

"Jacob, I'm coming down to get you!"

Then Victor shuffled along the edge of the cliff until he was facing the crowd. The onlookers were huddled and some were filming with their phones.

Tammy was standing at the front of the rescue line, holding the rope.

She shouted, "Okay, everyone, we're going to ease him down slowly."

Victor clung to the jagged cliff and held his breath. He felt himself being gently lowered through the air. Then, all of a sudden, he was dangling in the air over a deep canyon, the wind whipping around him. The rope jerked and he felt himself falling. He gasped and almost screamed.

"Slowly!" called Tammy. "Lower him slowly!"

Victor's head spun and he clutched the rope tightly until his hands ached.

Victor inhaled deeply for what felt like the first time ever and panic gave way to clear thinking. He forced himself to look down and that's when he saw Jacob's face. It was full of relief and trust, and Victor suddenly felt calm.

Those people up there would not let him fall. He was no longer the terrified child high in a tree. He was a park ranger who had a job to do.

He called out to Jacob, "It's okay, Jacob – everything's going to be just fine!"

A note from the author

National parks have many amazing locations and animals, but they can also be dangerous. Sometimes crowds of tourists are drawn to a particular location because someone has posted a photo on social media. Often, people take risks as they try to get the best photos.

I wanted to show how this might make the job of a park ranger difficult – they have to try and keep everyone safe, even the people risking their lives.